FIRST EXPERIENCES

ZACH'S FIRST VISIT TO THE ZOO

by Katie Chanez
illustrated by Daniela Massironi

GRASSHOPPER

Tools for Parents & Teachers

Grasshopper Books enhance imagination and introduce the earliest readers to fiction with fun storylines and illustrations. The easy-to-read text supports early reading experiences with repetitive sentence patterns and sight words.

Before Reading

- Look at the cover illustration. What do readers see? What do they think the book will be about?
- Look at the picture glossary together. Sound out the words. Ask readers to identify the first letter of each vocabulary word.

During Reading

- “Walk” through the book with the reader. Discuss new or unfamiliar words. Sound them out together.
- Look at the pictures together. Point out any labels.

After Reading

- Review the picture glossary again. Ask readers to locate the words in the text.
- Ask the reader: How did Zach feel when he had to wait to see the otters? How do you know?

Grasshopper Books are published by Jump!
3500 American Blvd W, Suite 150
Bloomington, MN 55431
www.jumplibrary.com

Jump! is a division of FlutterBee Education Group.

Library of Congress Cataloging-in-Publication Data

Names: Chanez, Katie, author.
Massironi, Daniela, illustrator.
Title: Zach's first visit to the zoo / by Katie Chanez; illustrated by Daniela Massironi.
Description: Minneapolis, MN: Jump!, Inc., 2026.
Series: First experiences
Audience: Ages 3–6.
Identifiers: LCCN 2024044340 (print)
LCCN 2024044341 (ebook)
ISBN 9798892138765 (hardcover)
ISBN 9798892138772 (paperback)
ISBN 9798892138789 (ebook)
Subjects: CYAC: Patience—Fiction. | Zoos—Fiction.
LCGFT: Picture books.
Classification: LCC PZ7.1.C4794 Zac 2026 (print)
LCC PZ7.1.C4794 (ebook)
DDC [E] —dc23
LC record available at https://lccn.loc.gov/2024044340
LC ebook record available at https://lccn.loc.gov/2024044341

Editor: Alyssa Sorenson
Direction and Layout: Molly Ballanger
Illustrator: Daniela Massironi

Printed in the United States of America at Corporate Graphics in North Mankato, Minnesota.

Table of Contents

Worth the Wait

Today is my first visit to the zoo!

"Look, Zach!" my sister says.
"Otters! Your favorite!"

"Let's go see the otters!" I say.

"We will," Dad says. "But there are other animals, too. Look."

"I want to see the otters now!" I shout.

"Be patient," Mom says.
"We will see them soon."

I take a deep breath.

I see chimps swing.

I see lions.

I see rays.

We touch them.

I see the otters!

The zoo is fun!

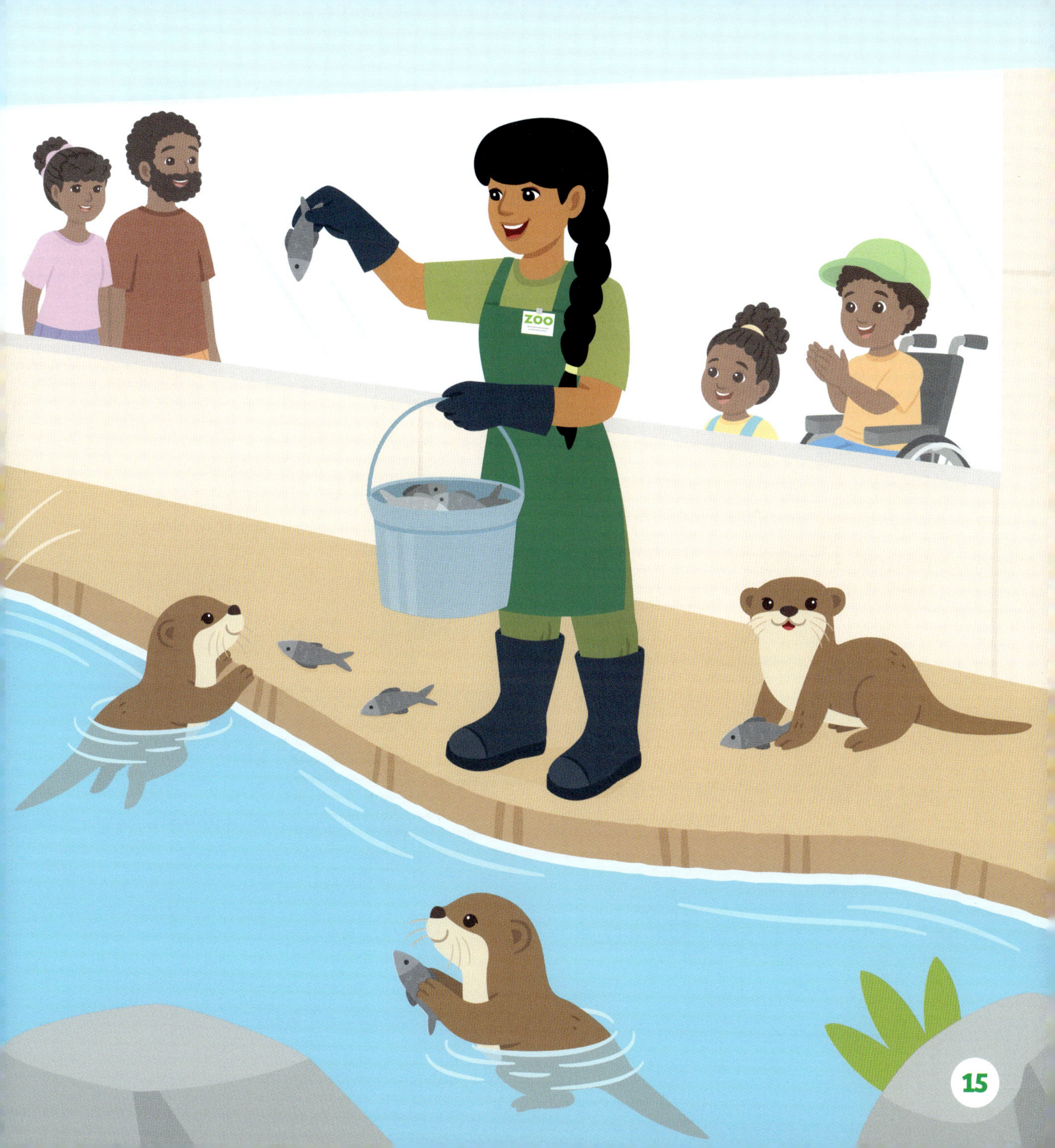
ZOO

Let's Review!

Zach feels impatient. How do we know?

A. He waits quietly. **B.** He politely asks to see the otters.
C. He has fun seeing the other animals. **D.** He shouts and bangs his fists.

Picture Glossary

favorite
The person or thing that one likes more than all others.

patient
Able to put up with problems and waiting without getting angry or upset.

shout
To speak or call out loudly.

visit
A short stay at a place.

Let's Review! Answer Key: **D.** He shouts and bangs his fists.